My name is ______________________

I am __________ years old.

I am in year ___________.

I like to ______________________________________

____

This is a picture of me.

Trace over

at at at at at

Copy

at

Trace over the letters.

Add at to finish the words.

at

a g

Trace over

ag ag ag ag ag

Copy

ag

Make the words and trace over the sounds.

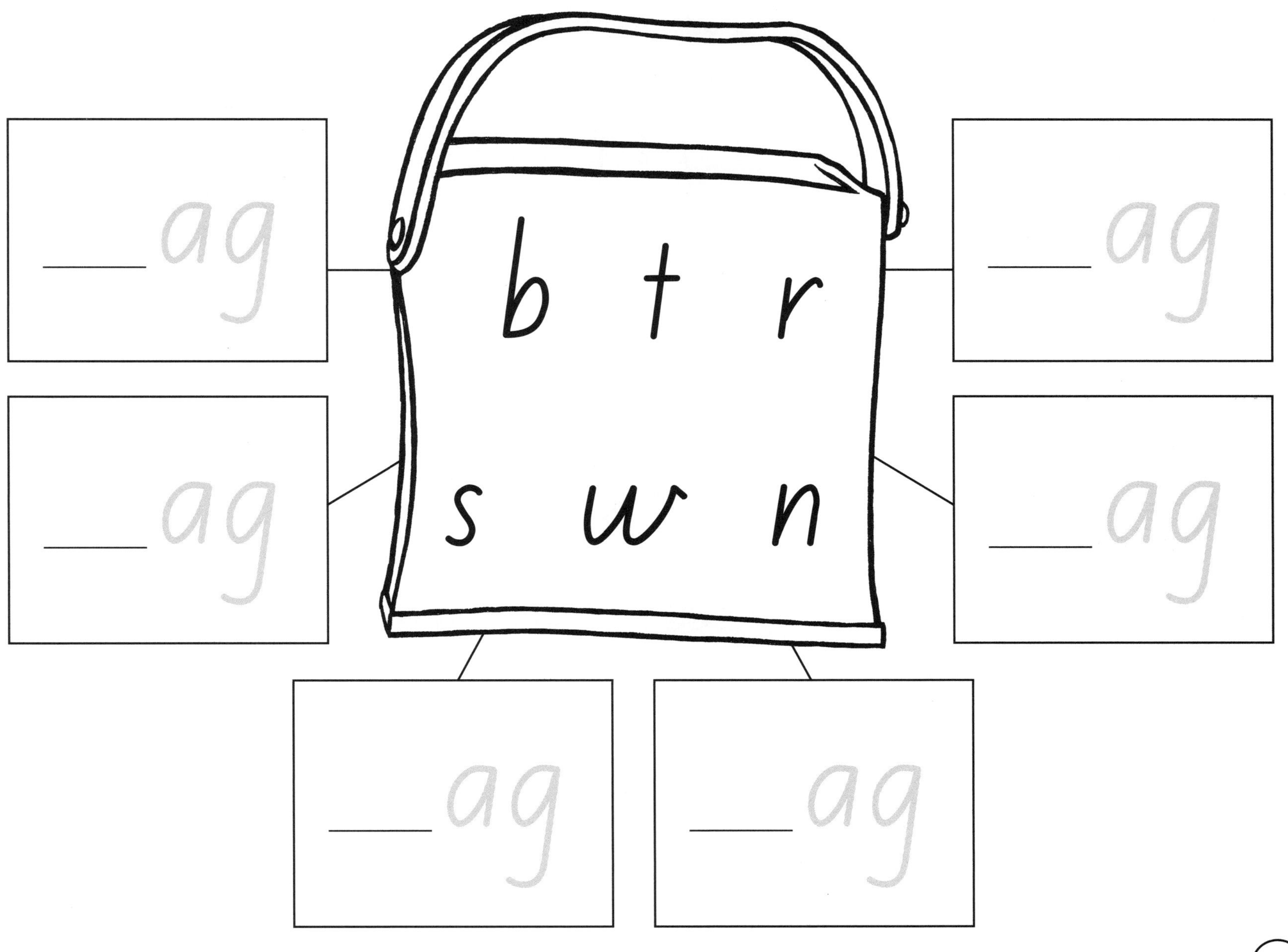

Trace over

an an an an an

Copy

an

Trace over the words.

ran

man

van

can

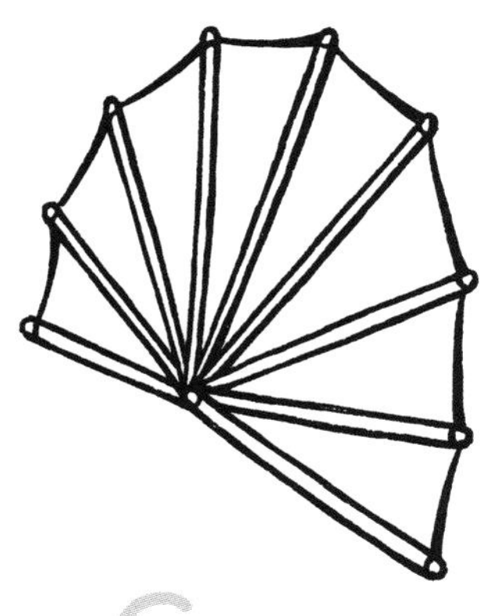

fan

pan

an

ap

Trace over

ap ap ap ap ap

Copy

Make *ap* words. One has been done for you.

c l m n t g

ap

cap

Trace over

ad ad ad ad

Copy

ad

Trace over the ad words.

Colour the ad words in the wordsearch.

Dad mad

pad had

bad lad

sad

p	a	d	m
s	a	d	a
h	D	a	d
a	b	a	d
d	l	a	d

ad

am

Trace over

am am am am

Copy

am

Trace over the letters. Add am to finish the words.

S__ __	P__ __	j__ __
__ __	d__ __	h__ __

Add am and read the sentences.

 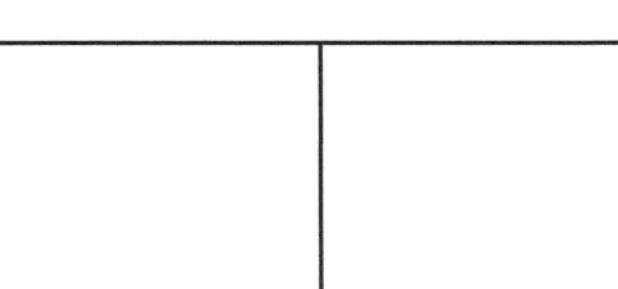 a boy.

My name is 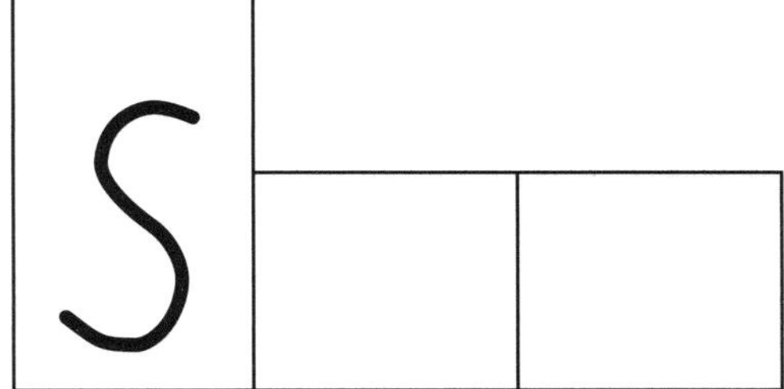 .

Trace over

et et et et et

Copy

et

Trace over the letters. Add et to finish the words.

et

Trace over

ed ed ed ed ed

Copy

ed

Make words and trace over the sounds.

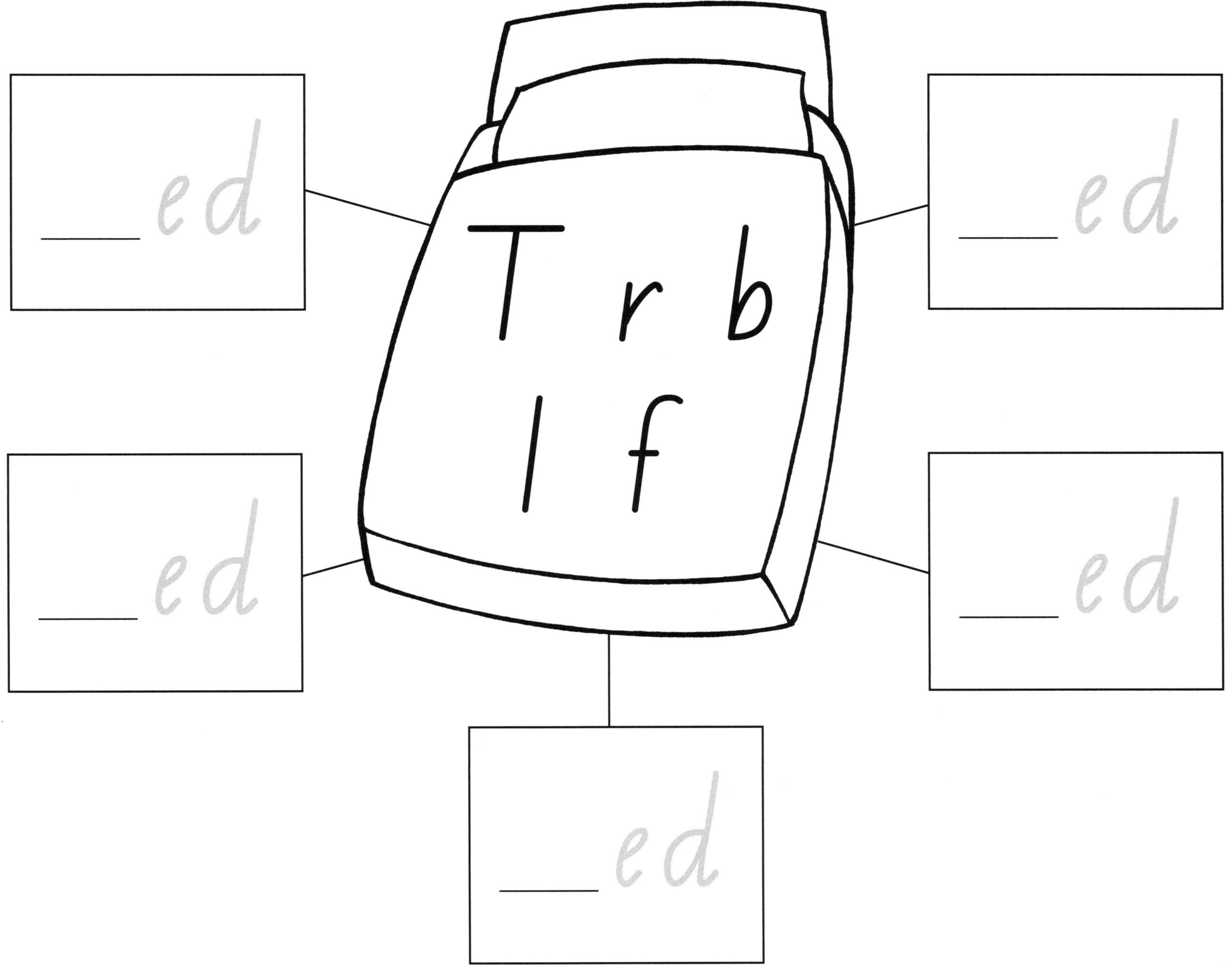

Trace over

en en en en en

Copy

en

Trace over the en words.

Look at the balloons. Can you write three boy's names?

en

eg

Trace over

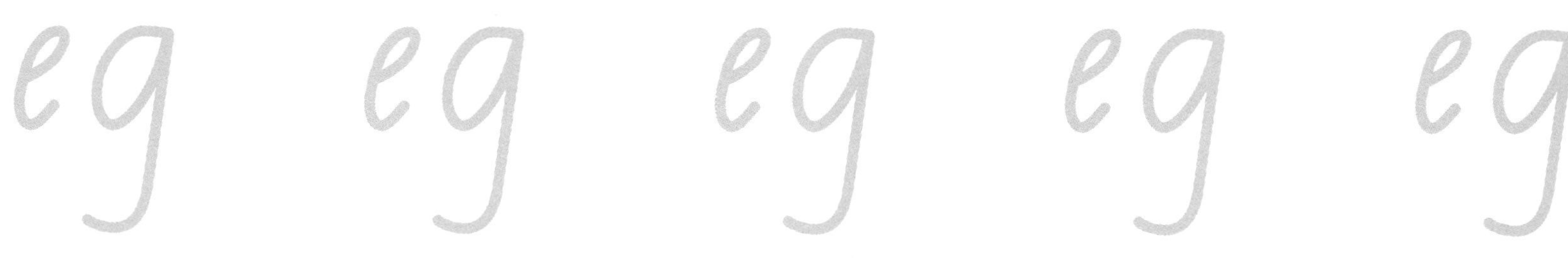

eg eg eg eg eg

Copy

eg

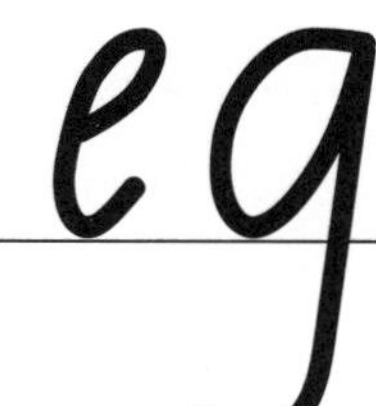

Write the eg words on the T-shirt.

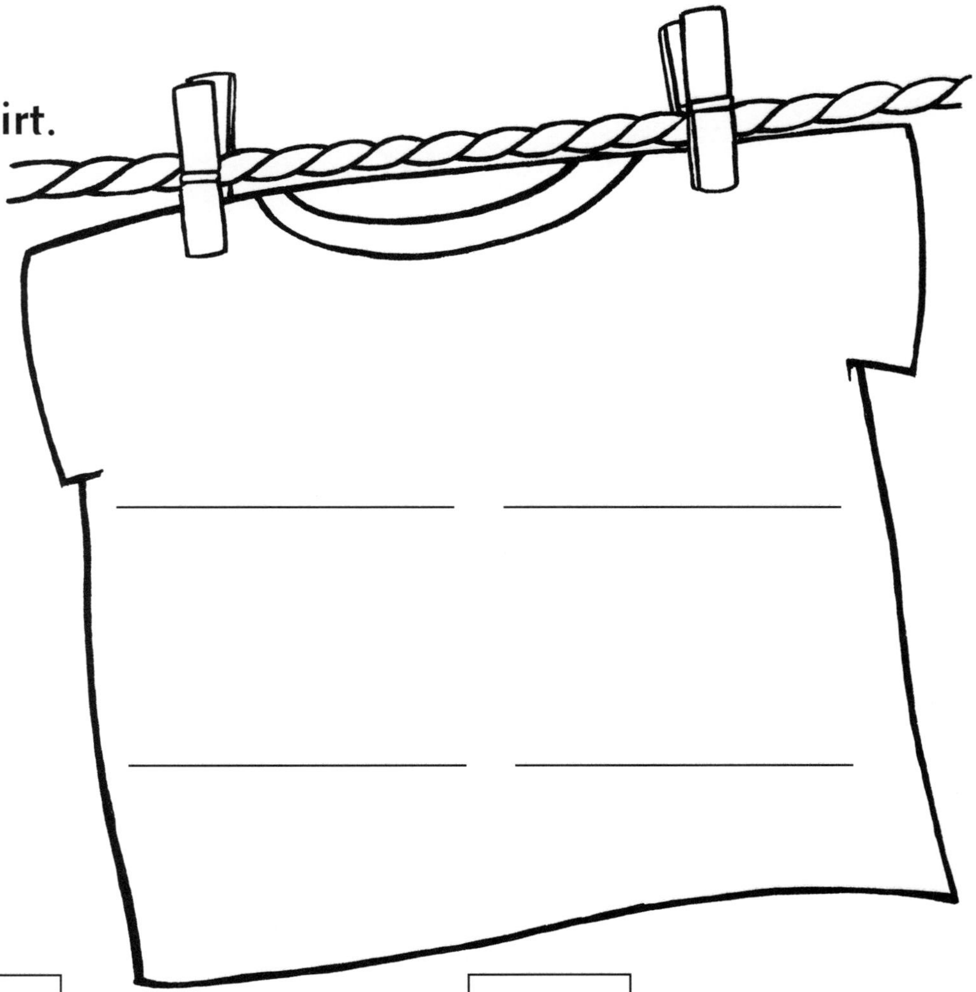

beg keg

leg peg

Add eg.

p

l

k

Trace over

Copy

Trace over the letters. Add it to finish the words.

K__ __

h__ __

m__ __

p__ __

s__ __

f__ __

b__ __

Add an it word to finish the sentence.

I can __ __ __ the ball.

it

Trace over

ig ig ig ig ig

Copy

ig

Make ig words. One has been done for you.

p d f b w j

ig

pig

Trace over

in in in in in

Copy

in

Trace over the letters.

Add in to finish the words.

Draw a picture for each word.

Hi!
My name is Lin.

b__ __

p__ __

t__ __

f__ __

in

Trace over

Copy

ip

Trace over the ip words. Colour the ip words in the wordsearch.

dip sip

tip lip

rip

d	i	p	t
r	i	p	i
m	s	i	p
l	i	p	o

Trace over

id id id id id

Copy

id

Trace over the id words.

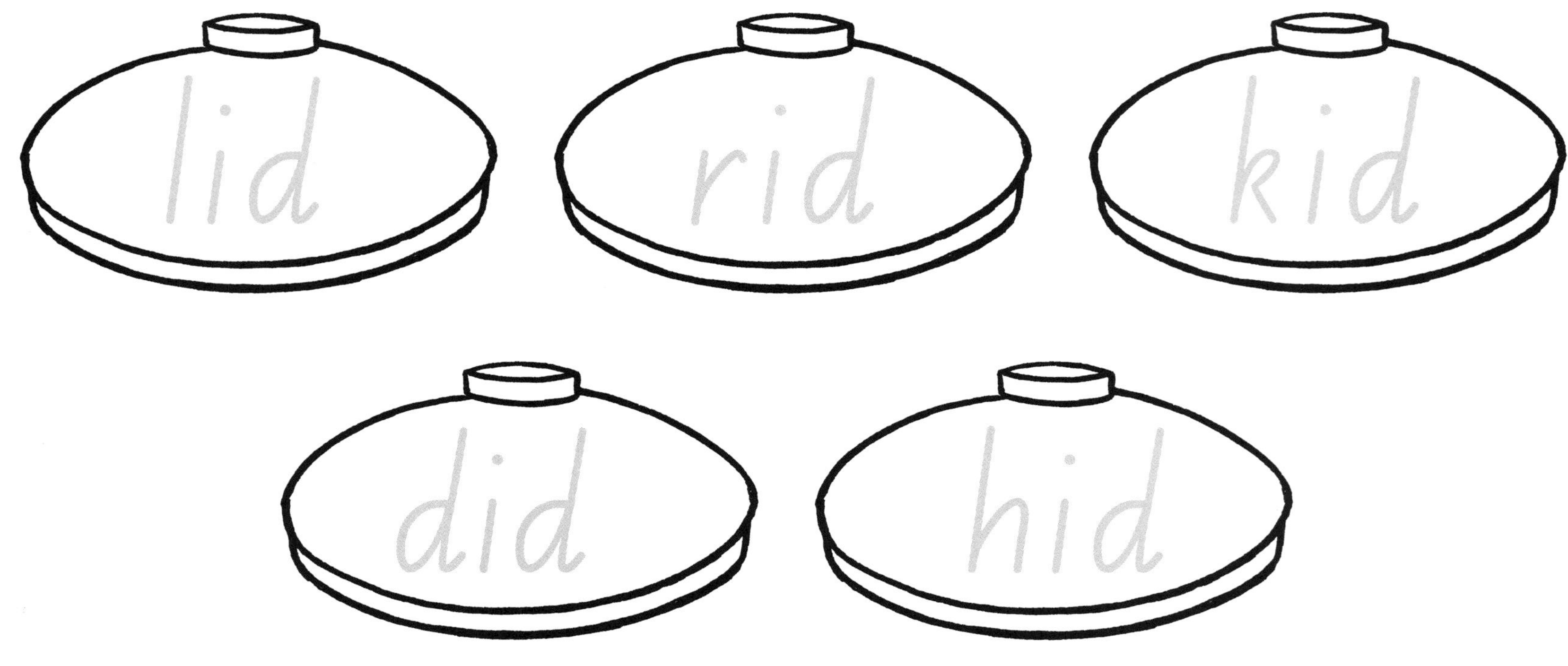

What am I?

I am a baby goat.

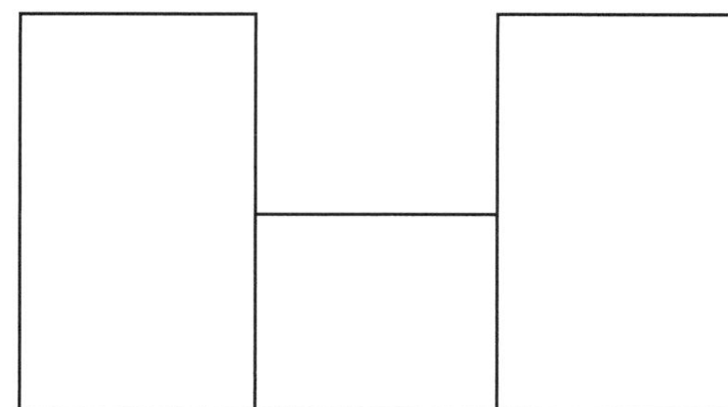

Draw me.

Trace over

ix ix ix ix

Copy

ix

Trace over the ix words. Colour the spaces with ix words red.

Are you six?

yes no

Trace over

ib ib ib ib ib

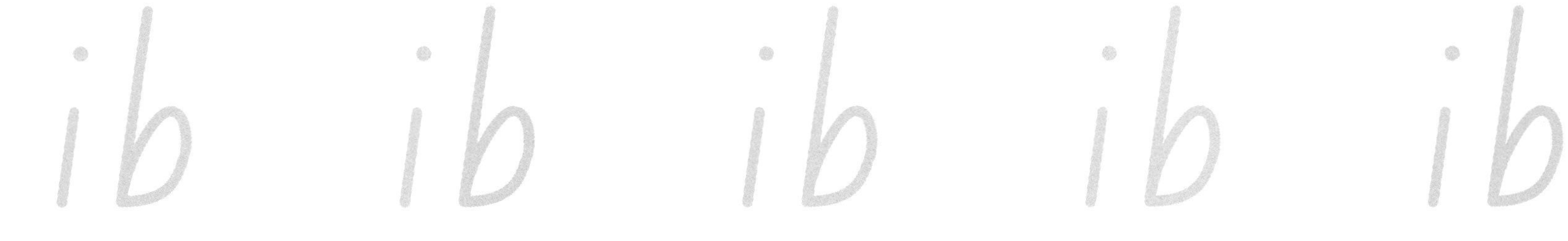

Copy

ib

Write ib words in the bib.

fix

hit

rib

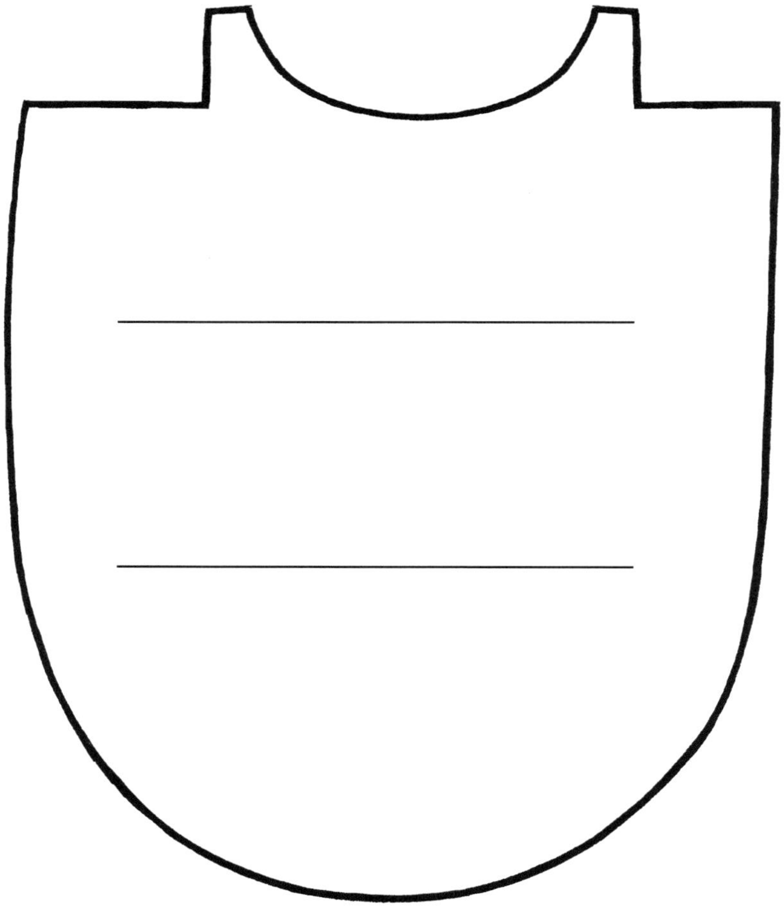

lid

bib

hip

Add ib.

r

f

b

ib

im

Trace over

im im im im

Copy

im

Trace over the letters. Add im to finish the words.

Draw Kim, Jim and Tim.

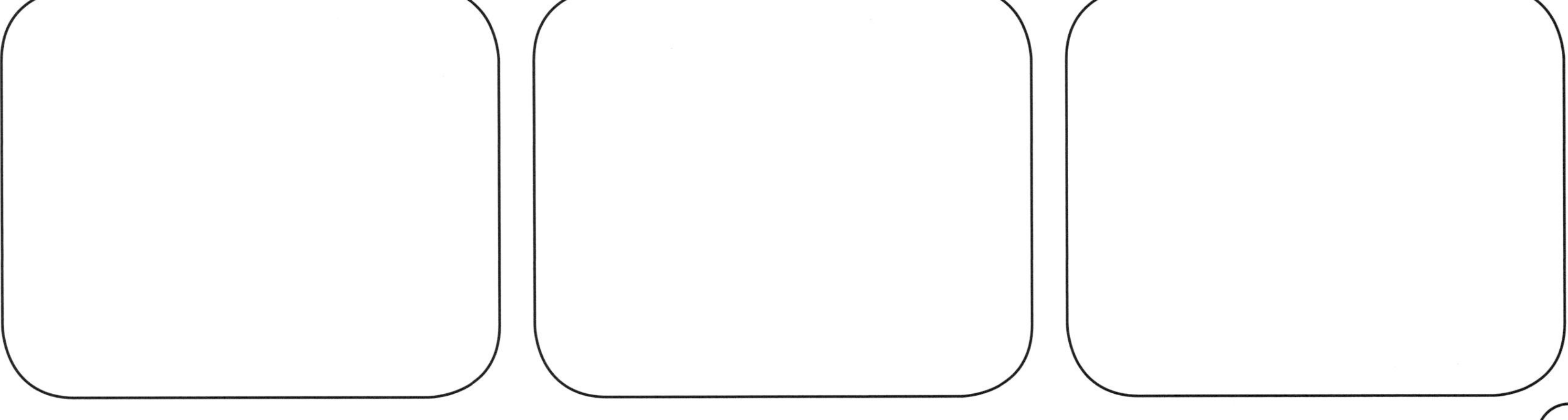

Trace over

ot ot ot ot ot

Copy

ot

Make ot words.

g d p n l c h

ot

ot

Trace over

og og og og og

Copy

og

Trace over the letters.

Add og to finish the words.

l___ ___

d___ ___

f___ ___

h___ ___

j___ ___

b___ ___

Trace over

od od od od od

Copy

od

Make the words and trace over the sounds.

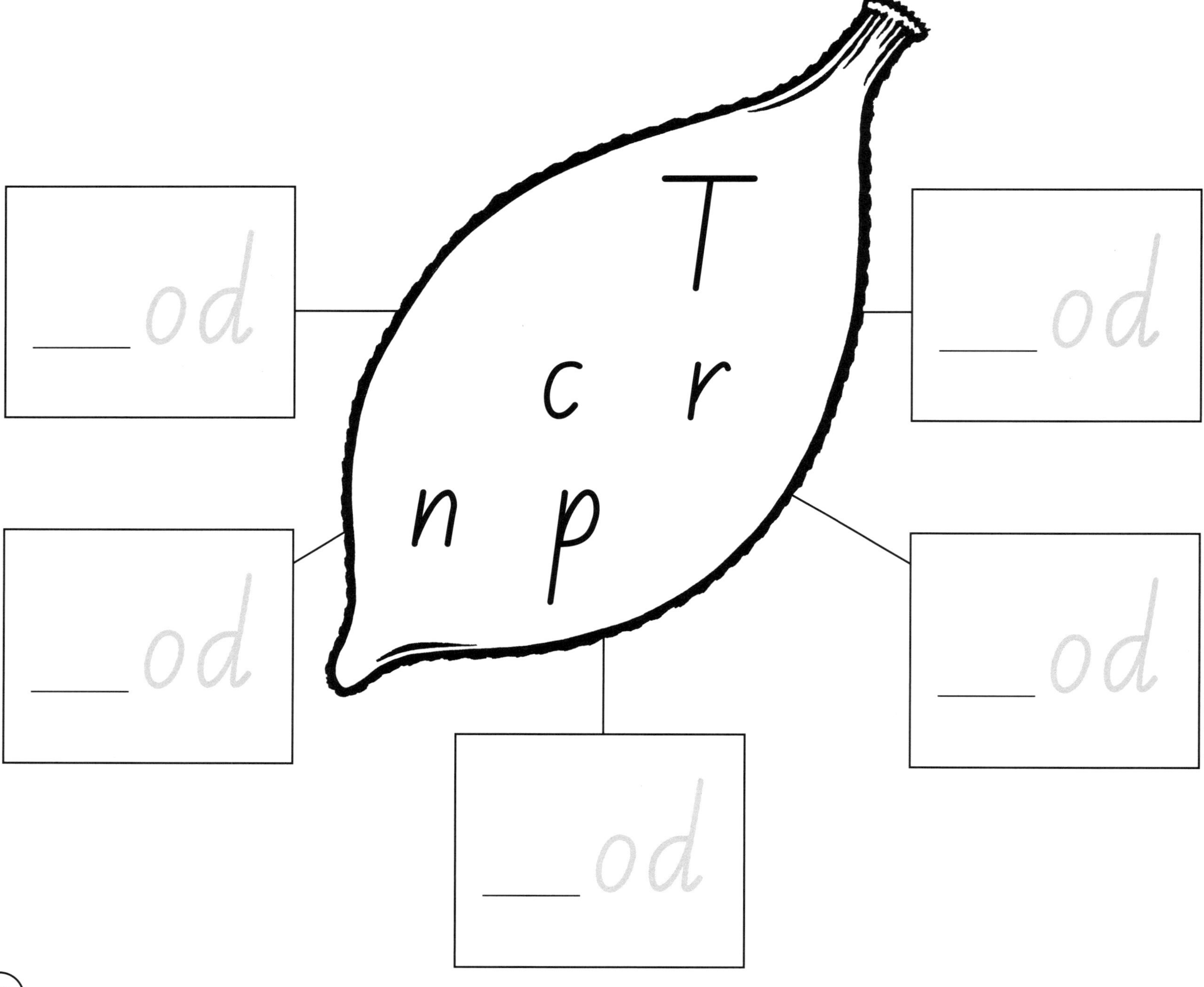

od

op

Trace over

op op op op op

Copy

op

Trace over the op words.

pop

top

lop

hop

mop

Trace over

Copy

ob

Trace over the ob words.

Colour the ob words in the wordsearch.

rob sob

Bob mob

job

j	o	b	r
B	o	b	o
l	s	o	b
m	o	b	c

ob

Trace over

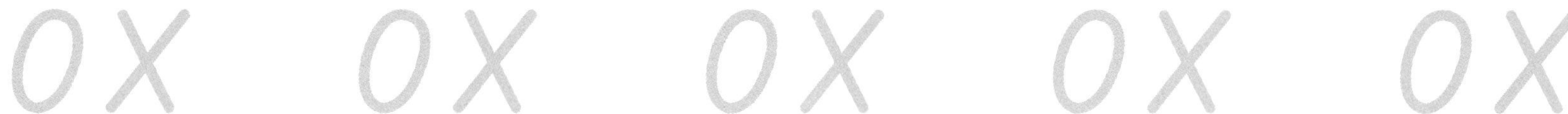

ox ox ox ox ox

Copy

ox

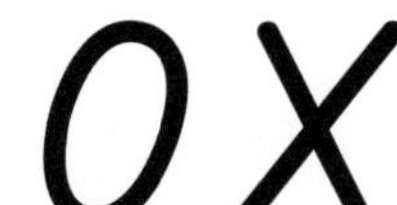

Write the ox words in the box.

Trace over any other words you know.

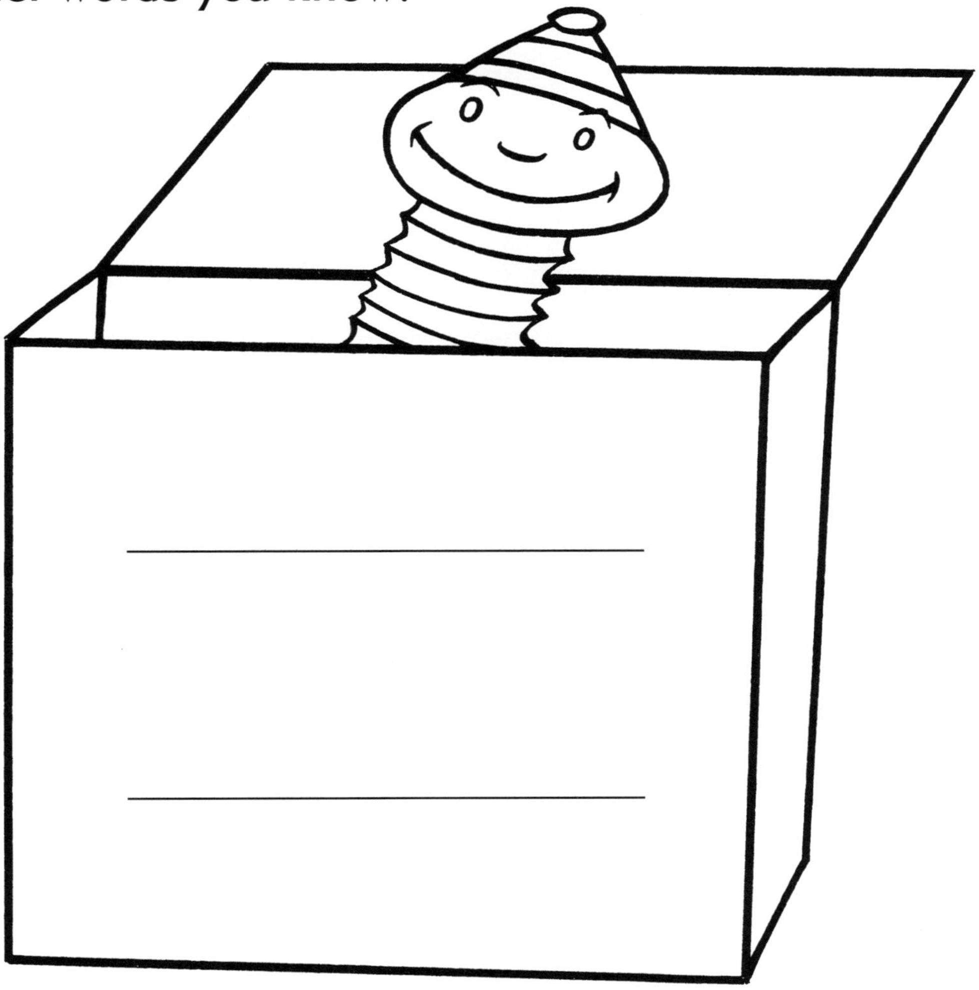

rob fog

dot Bob

box hot

pod fox

rod log

Trace over

un un un un un

Copy

un

Trace over the letters. Add un to finish the words.

Draw a picture for each word.

Add un and read the sentence.

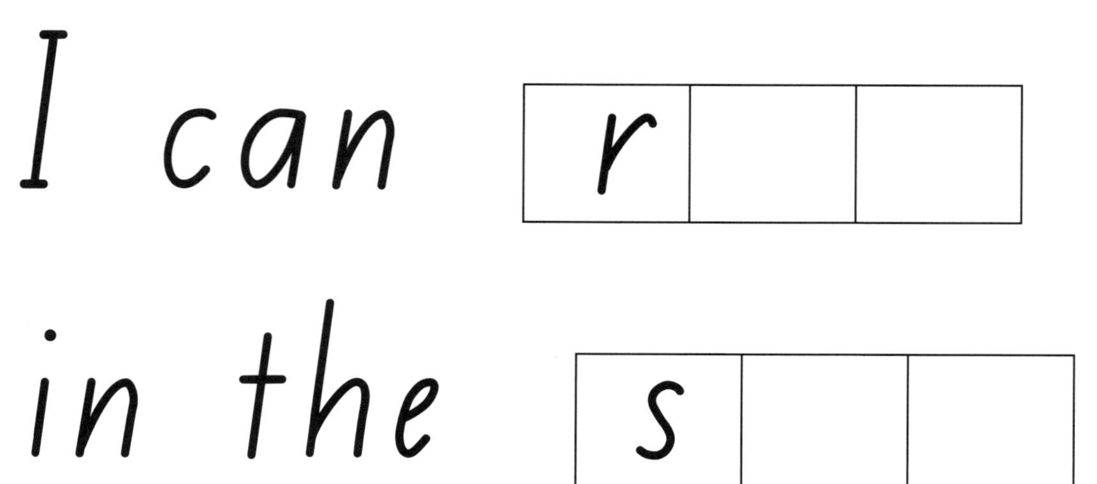

un

ut

Trace over

ut ut ut ut ut

Copy

ut

Make ut **words.**

Add ut.

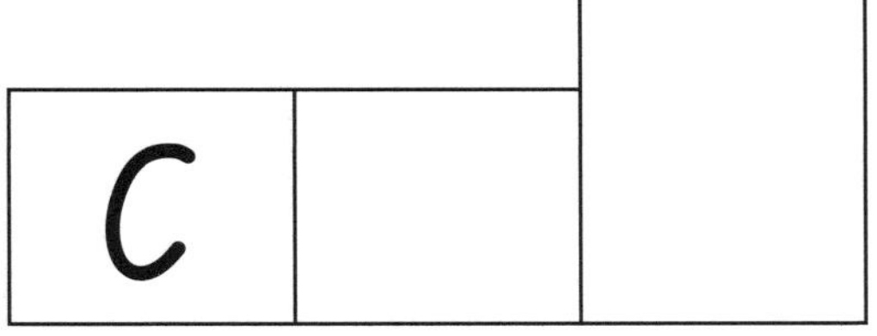

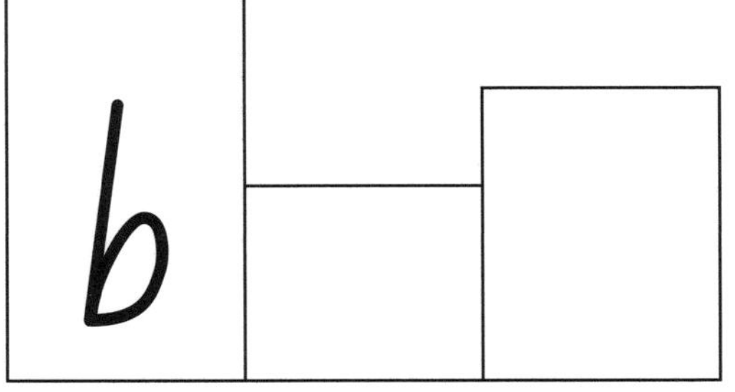

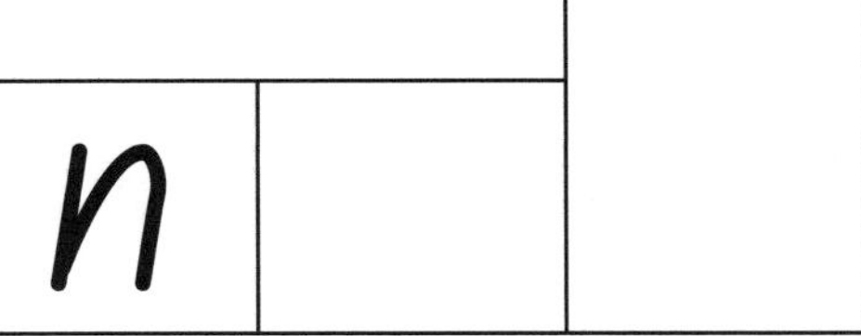

Trace over

ub ub ub ub

Copy

ub

Trace over the ub words.

Trace over the ub words in the poem.

Rub, rub, rub,

I'm in the tub!

ub

ud

Trace over

ud ud ud ud

Copy

ud

Write the ud words in the clouds.

rub bud

mud tub

Add ud and read the sentence.

I love to play in

the 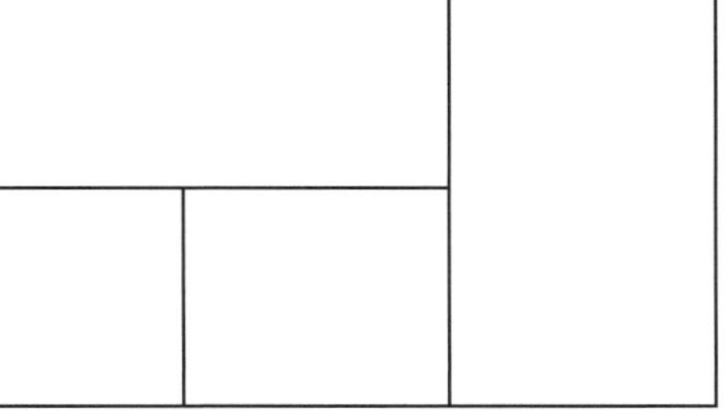 !

Trace over

ug ug ug ug ug

Copy

ug

Trace over the letters. Add ug to finish the words.

ug

um

Trace over

um um um um

Copy

um

Write the *um* words in the bee. Trace over other words you know.

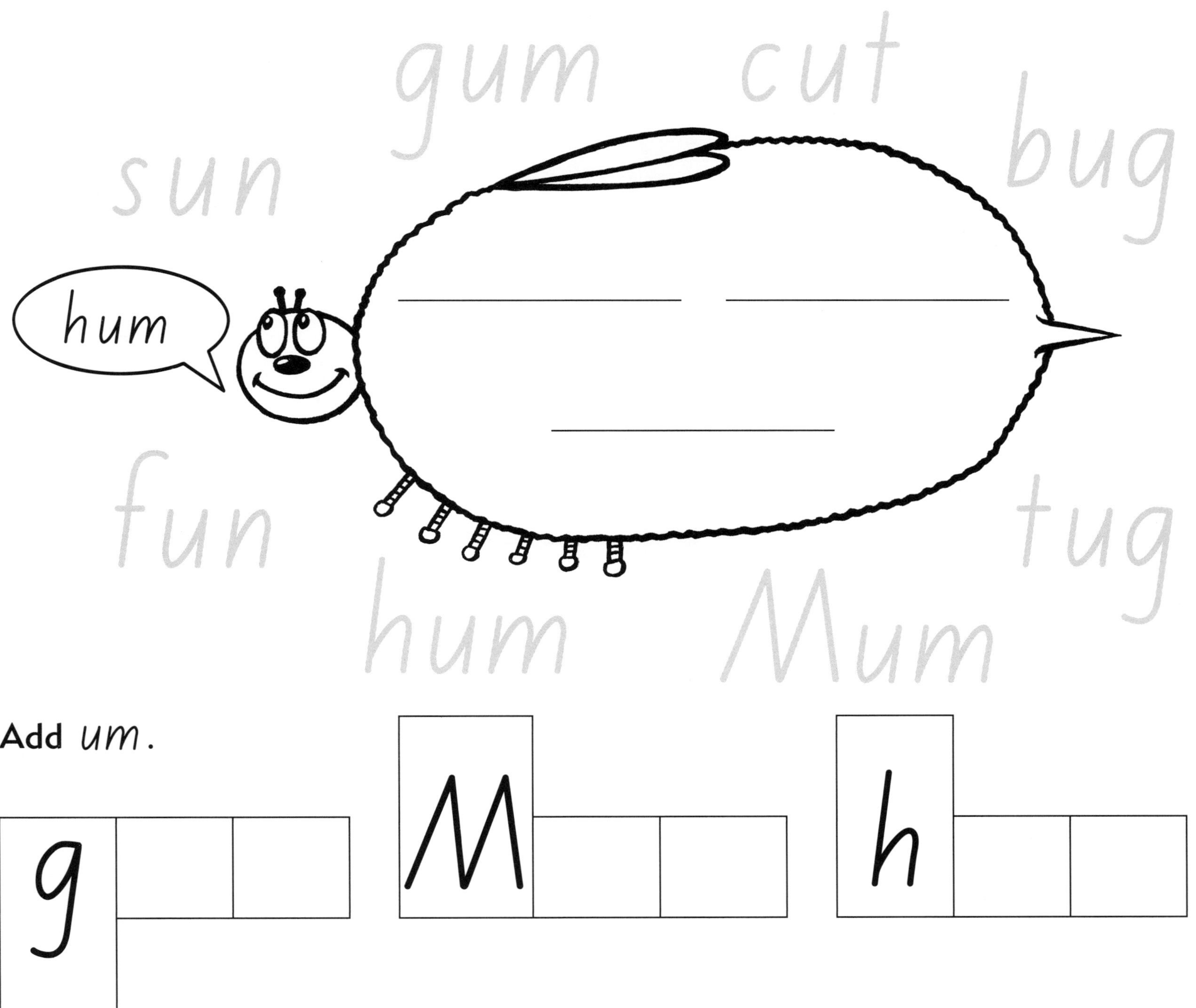

Add *um*.

Trace over

up up up up up

Copy

up

Trace over the letters. Add up to finish the words.

Draw a picture for each word.

c___ ___

p___ ___

Trace over the up words and read the sentence.

See the pup drink from a cup.

up

Trace over the sounds. Write three words for each sound.

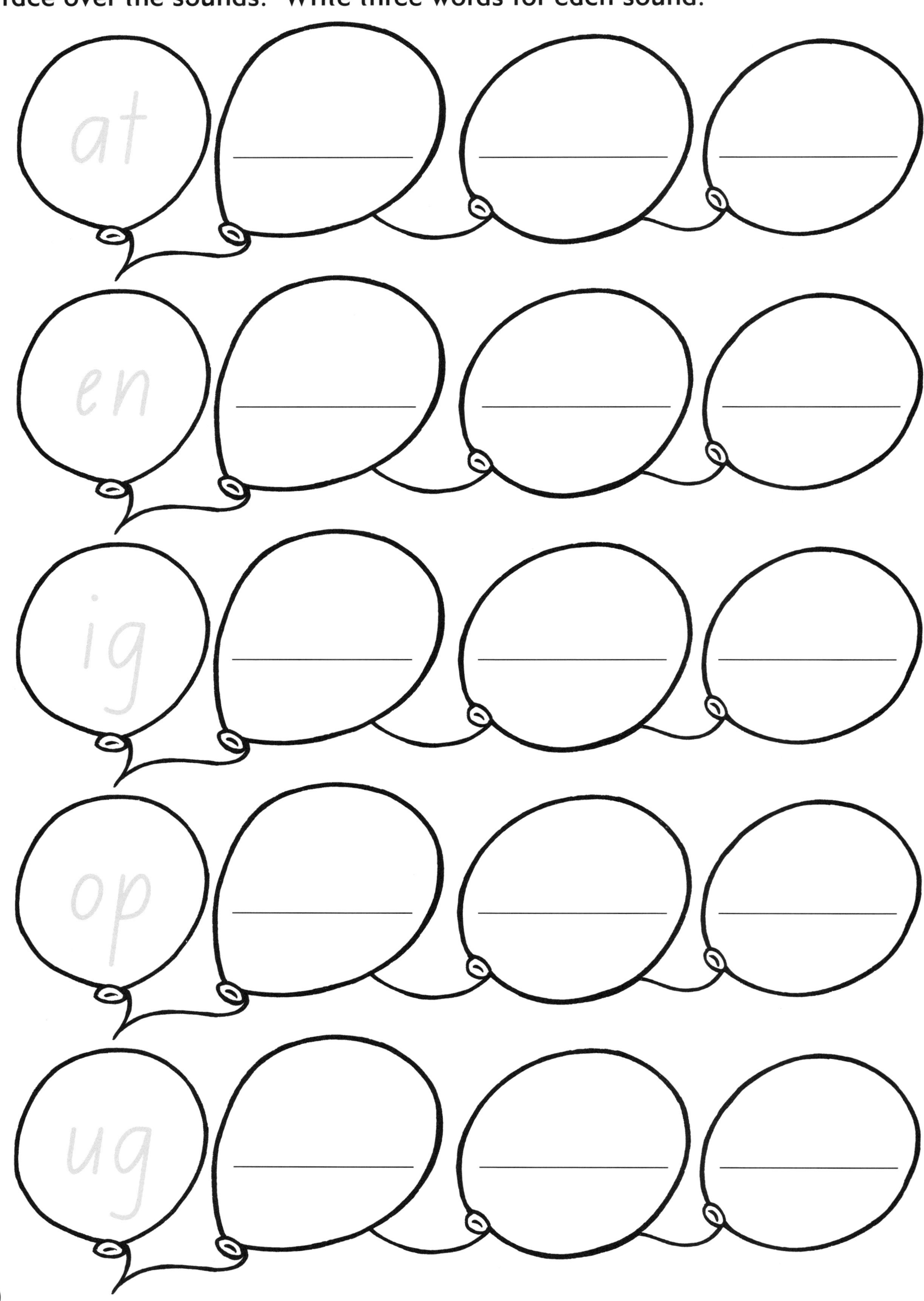